Lustige Sprachrätsel Englisch

Ab dem ersten Lernjahr

Hueber Verlag

3. 2. 1. | Die letzten Ziffern
2012 11 10 09 08 | bezeichnen Zahl und Jahr des Druckes.
Alle Drucke dieser Auflage können, da unverändert,
nebeneinander benutzt werden.
1. Auflage
Genehmigte Sonderausgabe für Hueber Verlag GmbH & Co. KG

Umschlaggestaltung: Parzhuber und Partner, München
Texte: Almuth Bartl
Illustrationen: Angela Weinhold
Druck und Bindung: Himmer AG, Augsburg
Gesamtherstellung: arsEdition GmbH, München
Printed in Germany
ISBN 978–3–19–009581–0

Vorwort

Die *Lustigen Sprachrätsel Englisch* sind kurzweilige, witzig illustrierte Sprachrätsel auf einfachem Niveau für zwischendurch und unterwegs. Sie bieten vergnügliches und unkompliziertes Wortschatzlernen und -wiederholen als Ergänzung zum Unterricht und für zu Hause. Abwechslungsreiche Übungstypen wie Bilderrätsel, Labyrinthe, Kreuzwort- und Silbenrätsel lassen keine Langeweile aufkommen. Die pfiffige „Miss Mouse" gibt Tipps und Hinweise zu den Übungen. Die einzelnen Übungsblätter kann man auch heraustrennen, die Lösungen befinden sich jeweils direkt auf der Rückseite. Das praktische Querformat ermöglicht, dass man auch in Bus und U-Bahn bequem auf dem Schoß rätseln kann.

Die *Lustigen Sprachrätsel* sind für Schüler ab dem ersten Lernjahr geeignet, ebenso für erwachsene Lernanfänger.

Viel Spaß beim „Sprachätseln"!

Full House

Die Namen der 10 abgebildeten Dinge findest du auch im Haus auf der Nachbarseite. Streiche die Wörter rechts mit Farbstift durch!

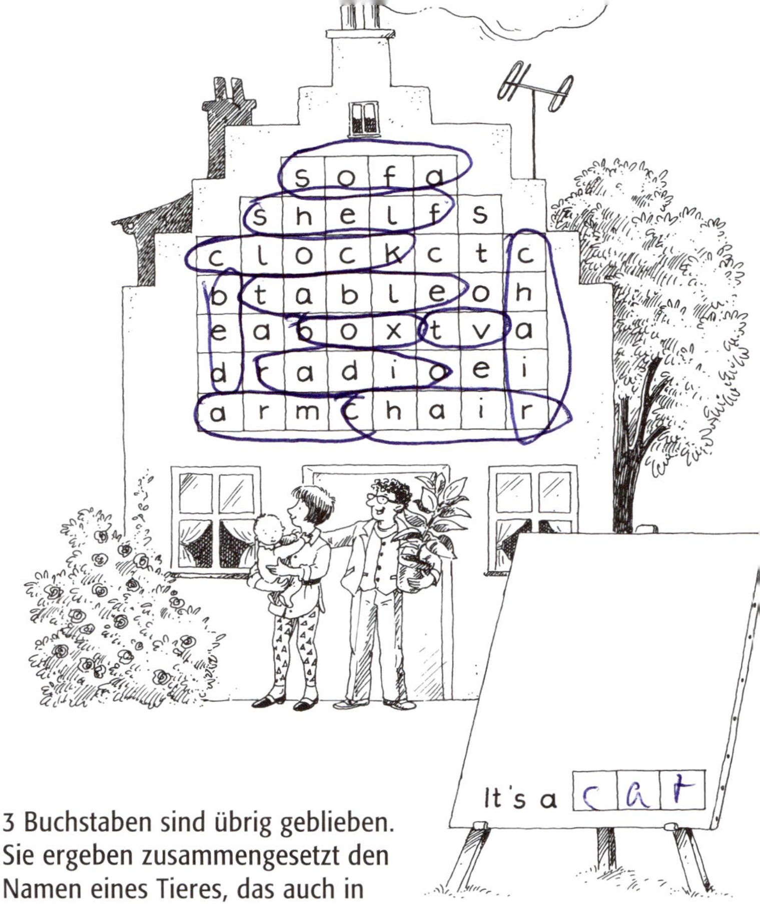

3 Buchstaben sind übrig geblieben. Sie ergeben zusammengesetzt den Namen eines Tieres, das auch in diesem Haus wohnt. Kannst du es auf die Tafel zeichnen?

		s	o	f	a		
	s	h	e	l	f	s	
c	l	o	c	k	c	t	c
b	t	a	b	l	e	o	h
e	a	b	o	x	t	v	a
d	r	a	d	i	o	e	i
a	r	m	c	h	a	i	r

Lösung: It’s a cat.

The scrambled crossword puzzle

Sortiere die Buchstaben und schreibe die richtigen Wörter in die Kästchen auf der rechten Seite.

1

n a k s e

2

o n i l

3

g i t r e

4

e s e h p

5

h e s r o

6

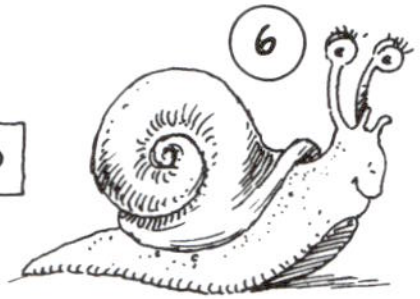

n a l i s

7

n a t

8

t a c

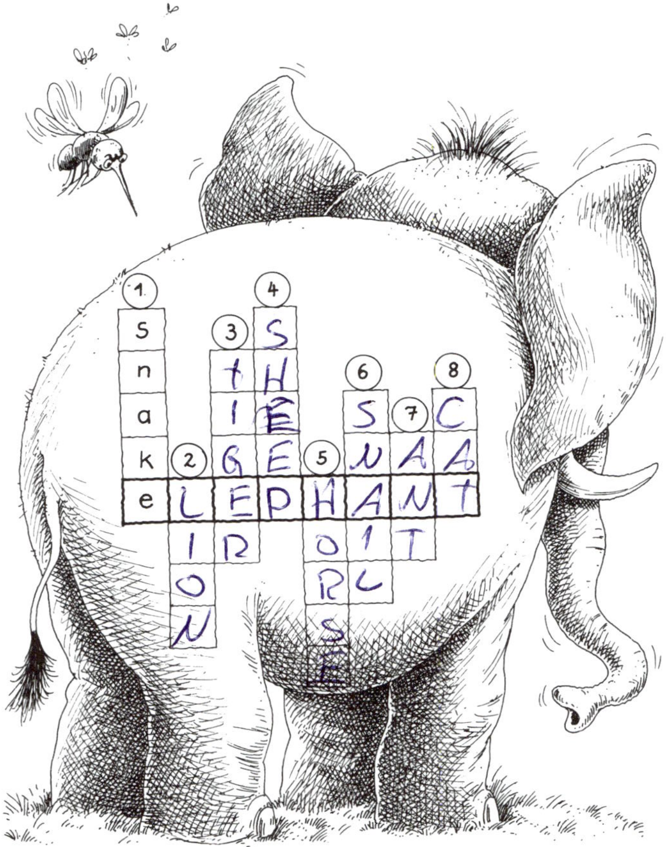

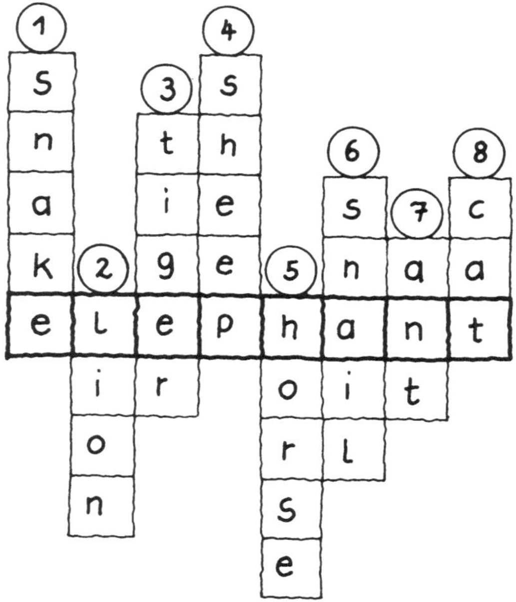
1 snake
2 lion
3 tiger
4 sheep
5 horse
6 snail
7 ant
8 cat
elephant

12 months in a year

Trage die jeweiligen Monatsnamen in das Rätselgitter ein!
Beispiel: 6th month (6. Monat) = June

12th month				D	E	C	E	M	B	E	R
3rd month					M	A	R	C	H		
7th month				J	U	L	Y				
9th month		S	E	P	T	E	M	B	E	R	
6th month				J	U	N	I				
2nd month						d					
	F	E	B	R	U	A	R	Y			
4th month				A	P	R	I	L			

Remember!
The months of the year are proper nouns. They always begin with a capital letter!

			D	e	c	e	m	b	e	r
				M	a	r	c	h		
			J	u	l	y				
	S	e	p	t	e	m	b	e	r	
			J	u	n	e				
					d					
F	e	b	r	u	a	r	y			
			A	p	r	i	l			

Where are the girls going to?

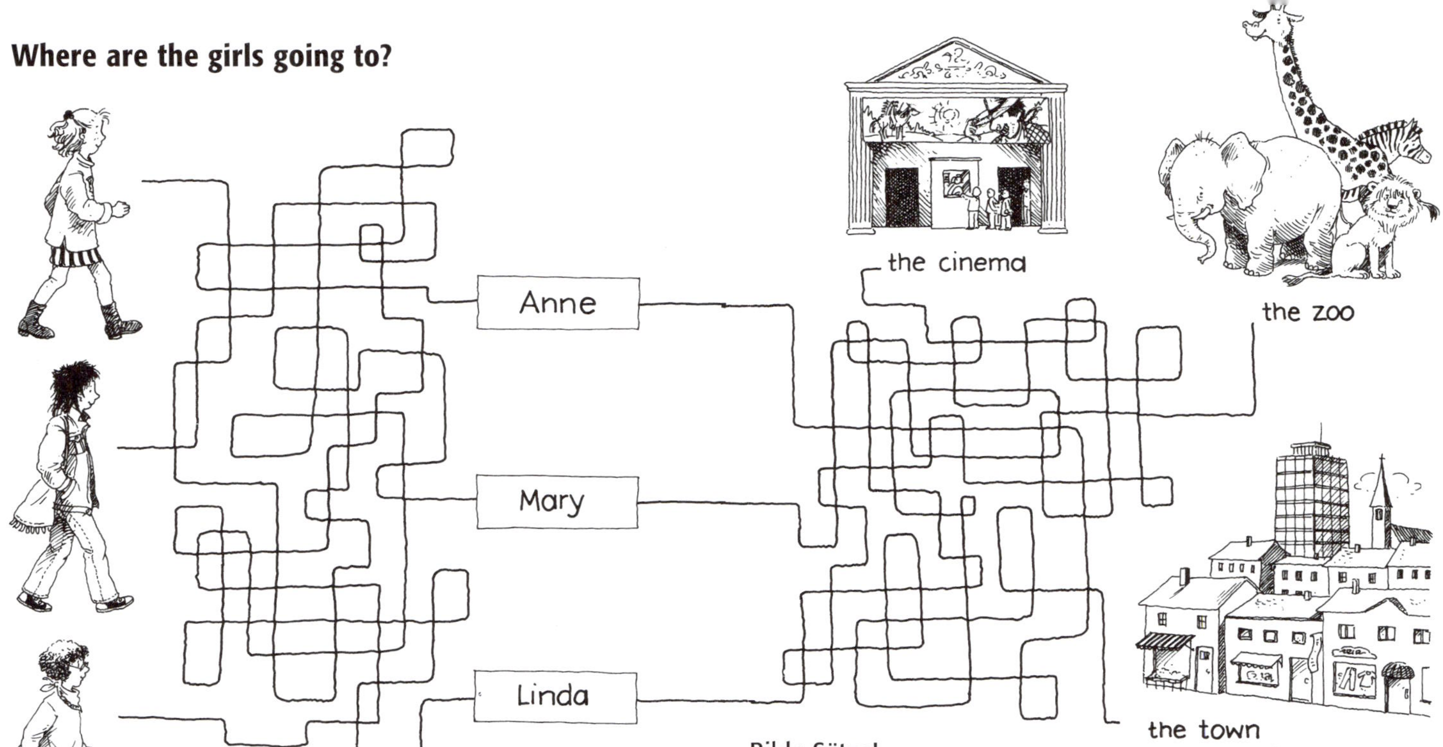

Bilde Sätze!

Anne is going to the cinema

Mary ______________________

Linda ______________________

Anne is going to the cinema.
Mary is going to town.
Linda is going to the zoo.

Clothes

Im Schrank findest du eine Menge Anziehsachen. Aber Vorsicht! 3 Dinge gehören nicht in den Kleiderschrank. Streiche sie durch!

sandwich
cake
bicycle

Who is who?

Miss Mouse, Mousey and Mike are good friends.

- Miss Mouse is not the smallest mouse.
- Mousey is not the first in line.
- Mike is smaller than Mousey.

Now, who is who?
Please write their names on the lines!

______ ______ ______

Parts of the body

Verbinde jedes Wort mit dem passenden Körperteil!

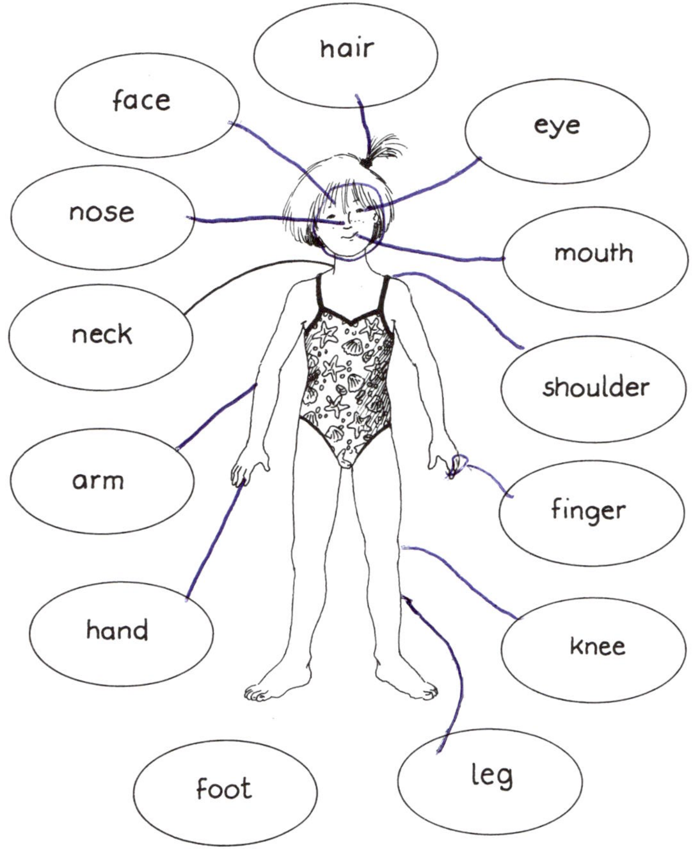

Miss Mouse – Mousey – Mike

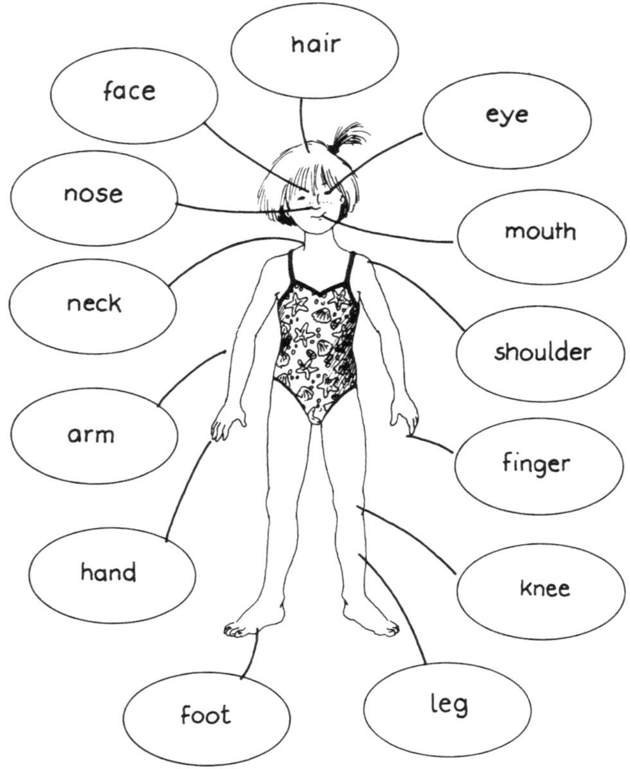

Family

How is Mike Grey related to Bill Grey? He is his

How is Kevin White related to Mary Grey? He is her

How is Charles Grey related to Bill Grey? He is his

How is Jane Grey related to Kevin White? She is his

How is Betty Grey related to Charles Grey? She is his

How is Diana Grey related to Bob Grey? She is his

Wenn du die dick umrandeten Buchstaben der Reihe nach hier einträgst, erhältst du den Namen von Baby Grey!

M

Mike Grey is Bill Grey's father.
Kevin White is Mary Grey's uncle.
Charles Grey is Bill Grey's brother.
Jane Grey is Kevin White's sister.
Betty Grey is Charles Grey's mother.
Diana grey is Bob Grey's aunt.

Baby Grey's name is Maureen.

Numbers

Male jedes Kästchen mit einer der folgenden Zahlen aus, und du erhältst ein Bild!

eighty-eight, thirty-five, twenty-five, seventy-five, seventy-three, fifty-nine, seventy-eight, eighty-three, seventy-two, fifteen, fifty-eight, sixty-five, thirty-eight, ninety-four, sixteen, forty-five, fifty-five, seventy-four, seventy-seven, ninety-seven, seventy-six, ninety-five, seventy-nine, five, twenty-seven, fifty-seven, forty-nine, ninety-six, fifty-six

1	2	3	4	5	6	7	8	9	10
11	12	13	14	15	16	17	18	19	20
21	22	23	24	25	26	27	28	29	30
31	32	33	34	35	36	37	38	39	40
41	42	43	44	45	46	47	48	49	50
51	52	53	54	55	56	57	58	59	60
61	62	63	64	65	66	67	68	69	70
71	72	73	74	75	76	77	78	79	80
81	82	83	84	85	86	87	88	89	90
91	92	93	94	95	96	97	98	99	100

- ★ a car
- ★ a sailing boat
- ★ a plane
- ★ a bicycle

You can see a sailing boat.

Dinosaurs

Brontosaurus hat 15 Wörter verschluckt, die mit dem Buchstaben „c" beginnen. Kannst du sie entdecken?

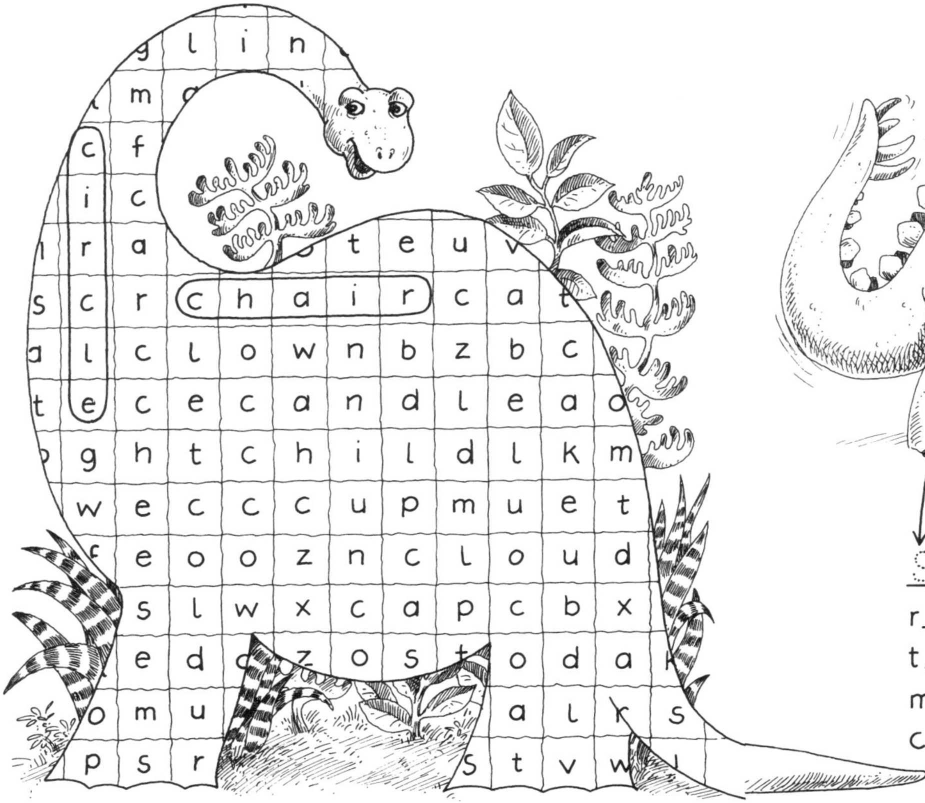

Mit den Buchstaben auf Stegosaurus kannst du die Wörter unten vervollständigen.

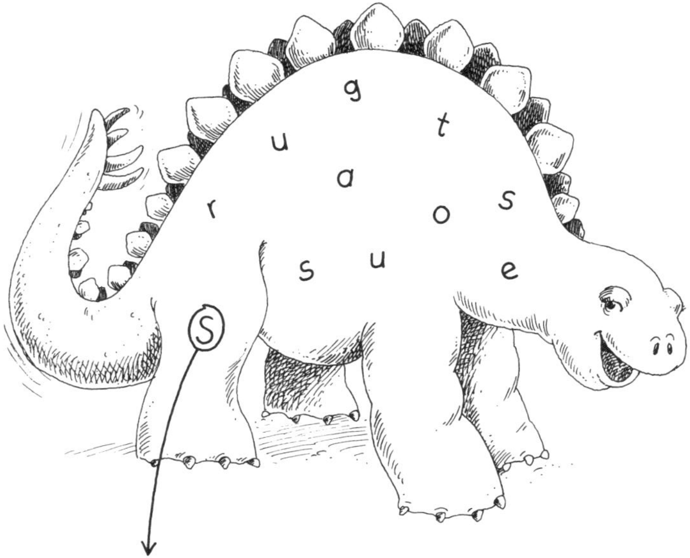

S̲unday
r__ler
t__ee
mo__se
c__r

b__d
hor__e
__irl
b__y
__able
chee__e

Sunday
ruler
tree
mouse
car
bed
horse
girl
boy
table
cheese

What does Miss Mouse do?

Suche die Verben im Buchstabengitter, kreise sie ein und schreibe sie unter die passenden Bilder.

Achtung!
He, she, it, das „s“ muss mit!
Schreibe also z. B.: she drinks

she cries

she p s

she

Wenn du alles richtig gemacht hast, bleiben im Gitter 7 Buchstaben übrig. Bilde daraus 2 weitere Verben und schreibe sie hier neben die deutsche Bedeutung!

warten – to

sehen – to

l	i	s	t	e	n	w	w
a	i	c	l	e	a	n	r
s	l	e	e	p	e	d	i
r	p	l	a	y	a	r	t
e	c	r	y	t	t	e	e
a	d	r	i	v	e	a	r
d	s	f	e	e	d	m	u
t	h	i	n	k	e	e	n

warten – to wait
sehen – to see

she writes
she cleans
she reads
she thinks
she drives

l	i	s	t	e	n	w	w
a	i	c	l	e	a	n	r
s	l	e	e	p	e	d	i
r	p	l	a	y	a	r	t
e	c	r	y	t	t	e	e
a	d	r	i	v	e	a	r
d	s	f	e	e	d	m	u
t	h	i	n	k	e	e	n

she plays
she sleeps
she eats
she listens
she dreams
she feeds
she runs

Opposites

Kennst du das Gegenteil?

Trage die dick umrandeten Buchstaben der Reihe nach hier ein!

☐☐☐ ☐☐☐ ☐ ☐☐☐☐ !

fast – slow
sad – happy
right – left
last – first
near – far
over – under

open – closed
cold – hot
good – bad
false – true
light – heavy
off – on
long – short
winter – summer

Lösung: You are a star!

On the farm

Weißt du die Namen der abgebildeten Tiere und Gegenstände? Sie beginnen alle mit dem Buchstaben „h“.

1	h									
2	h									
3	h									
4	h									
5	h									
6	h									
7	h									
8	h									
9	h	o	r	s	e					
10	h									
11	h									
12	h									

1	h	e	n							
2	h	a	t							
3	h	u	t							
4	h	a	y							
5	h	a	n	d						
6	h	a	i	r						
7	h	o	r	n						
8	h	o	u	s	e					
9	h	o	r	s	e					
10	h	a	m	m	e	r				
11	h	a	m	s	t	e	r			
12	h	e	l	i	c	o	p	t	e	r

Words with -oo

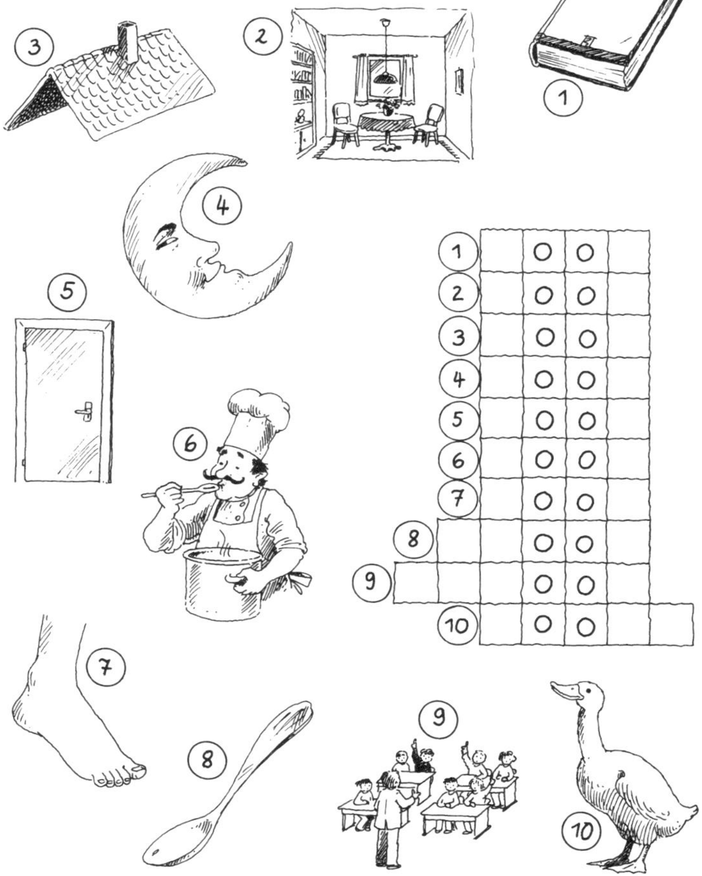

Words with -ee

1. book
2. room
3. roof
4. moon
5. door
6. cook
7. foot
8. spoon
9. school
10. goose

1. bee
2. beer
3. tree
4. feet
5. geese
6. teeth
7. sheep
8. cheese
9. three
10. queen

Horses

Der Bauer ist nicht da. Deshalb soll Sam heute die Pferde in ihre Boxen bringen. Aber welches Pferd kommt wohin? Kannst du helfen? Verbinde!

Wenn du alles richtig machst, sagen dir die Buchstaben auf den Pferden, was mit dem Bauern los ist.

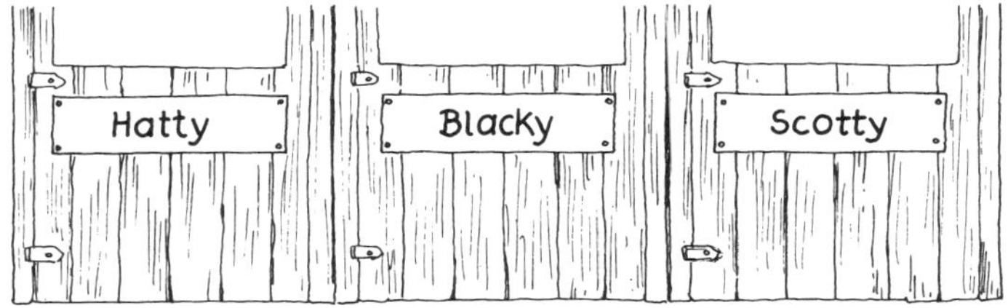

Lösung: He is ill.

Tom's room

cat	pencil	ball	goose	shoes	poster
radio	lamp	bed	chair	elephant	flag
scissors	satchel	table	trousers	toy car	
blanket	apple	window	carpet	glass	
plate	T-shirts	train	straw	book	

Trage die Anfangsbuchstaben der 5 ausgestrichenen Wörter hier ein!

You are ☐☐☐☐☐ !

goose
radio
elephant
apple
train

Lösung: You are great!

Butterflies

Wenn du die Wörter auf den Flügeln der Schmetterlinge ergänzt und die hinzugefügten Buchstaben zusammen liest, weißt du, wonach die Schmetterlinge suchen.

The butterflies are looking for ...

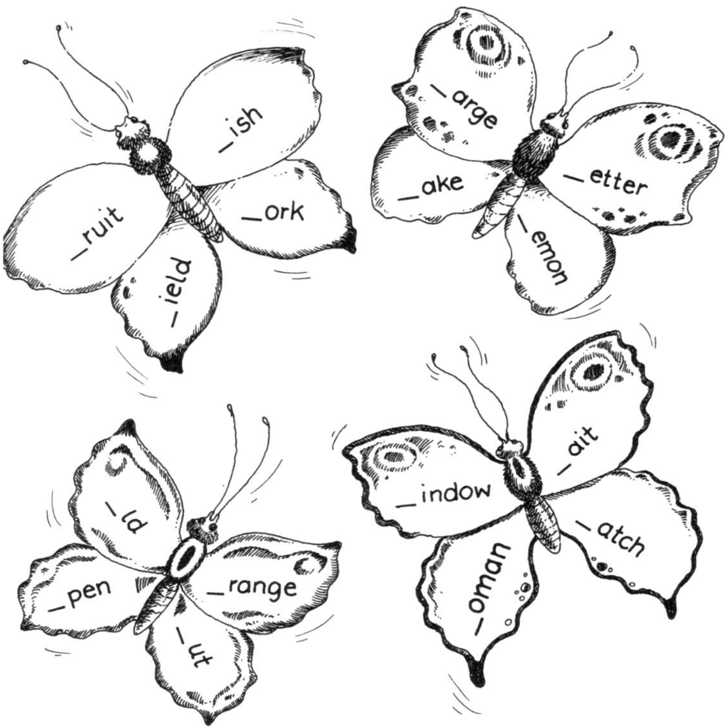

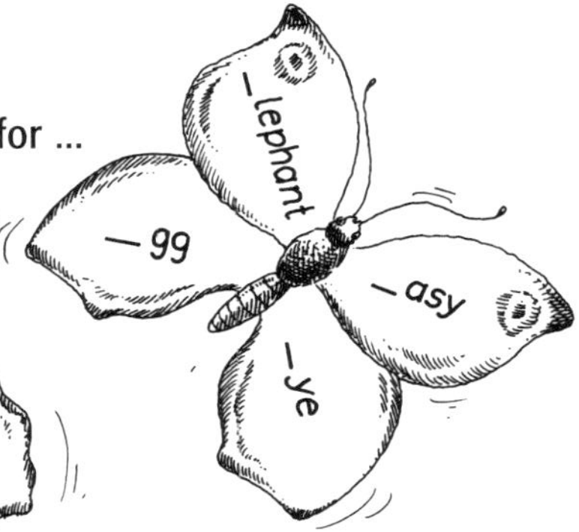

fruit	large	river	elephant
fish	letter	ruler	easy
field	lake	rain	egg
fork	lemon	run	eye
old	window		sweet
orange	wait		some
open	woman		satchel
out	watch		snake

Lösung:
The butterflies are
looking for flowers.

Let's rhyme!

Male alle Blasen mit Wörtern, die sich reimen, in derselben Farbe aus!

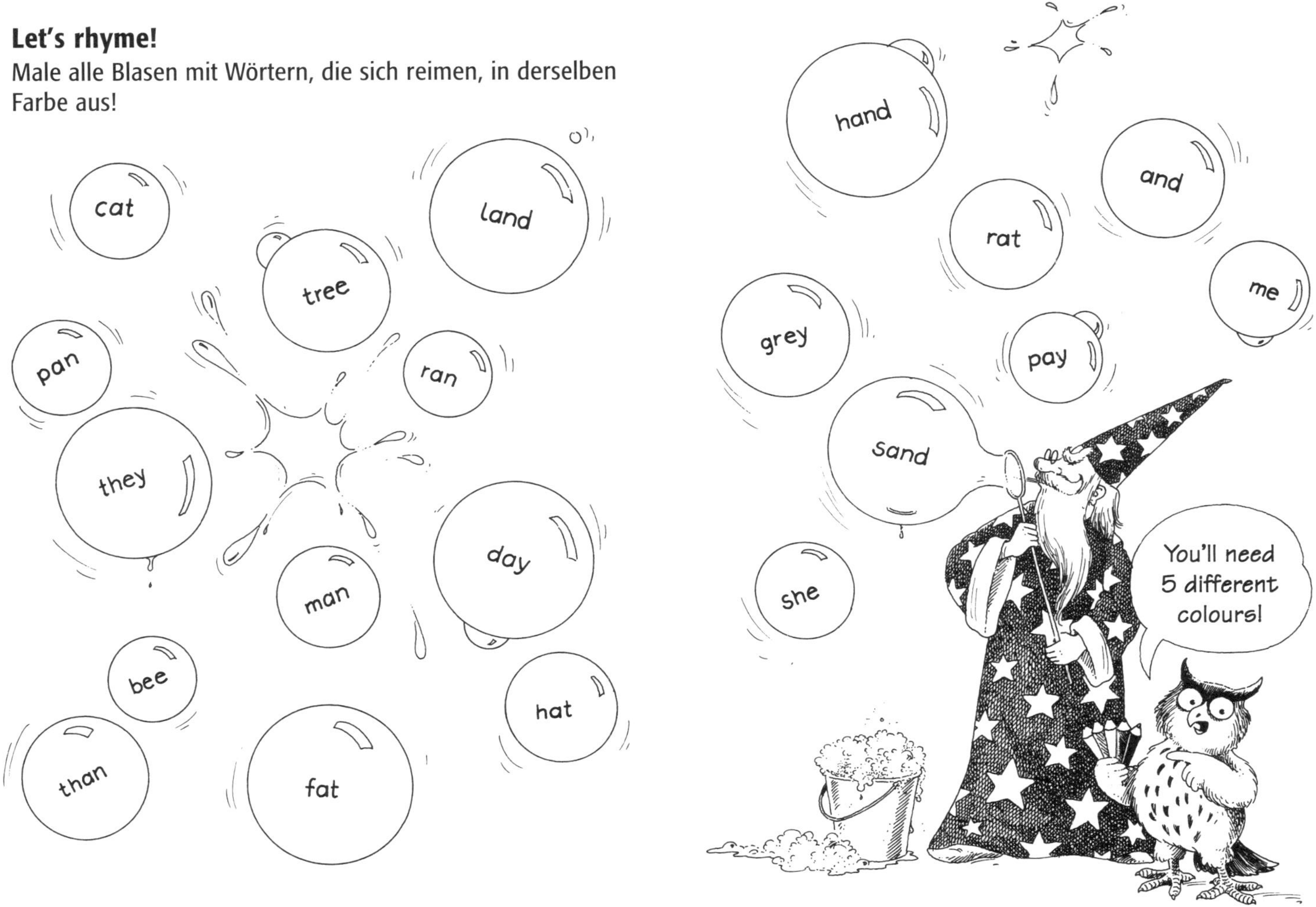

cat	tree	land	ran	they
hat	bee	hand	pan	grey
fat	me	sand	man	pay
rat	she	and	than	day

At the airport

Die Flugzeuge fliegen zu großen englischen, amerikanischen oder australischen Städten. Ordne die Buchstaben und kreise die 8 richtigen Städte ein!

Atlanta	Canberra	Washington	Manchester	Sydney	
Bristol	Aberdeen	Denver	London	Chicago	Adelaide
New York	Perth	Leeds	Dallas	Glasgow	

The aeroplanes go to:

Washington
Canberra
New York
Sydney
Manchester
London
Chicago
Leeds

Nouns and verbs

Schreibe das passende Verb unter das Bild!

verbs:

smell drive sleep draw write cut read drink

watch sit wear play cook ride

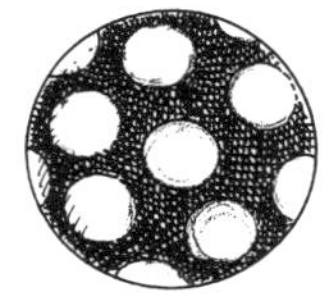

drive

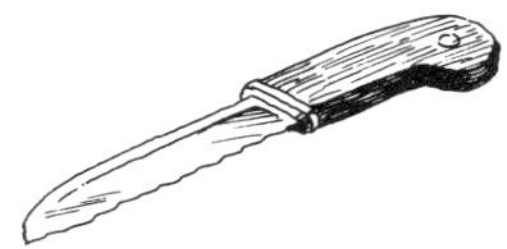

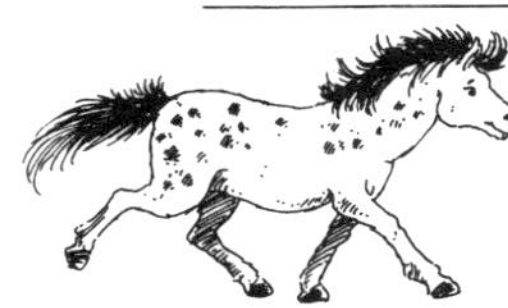

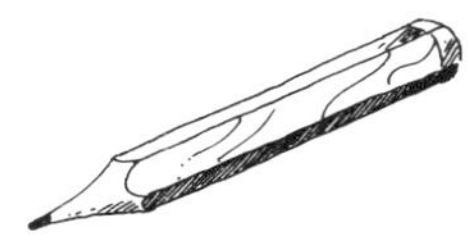

car – drive
bed – sleep
picture – draw
nose – smell
clothes – wear
chair – sit

ball – play
TV – watch
pot – cook
tea – drink
knife – cut
book – read
horse – ride
pencil – write

Miss Mouse is missing

Trage die entsprechenden Begriffe in das Rätselgitter ein,
und du erfährst, wo sich Miss Mouse versteckt hat!

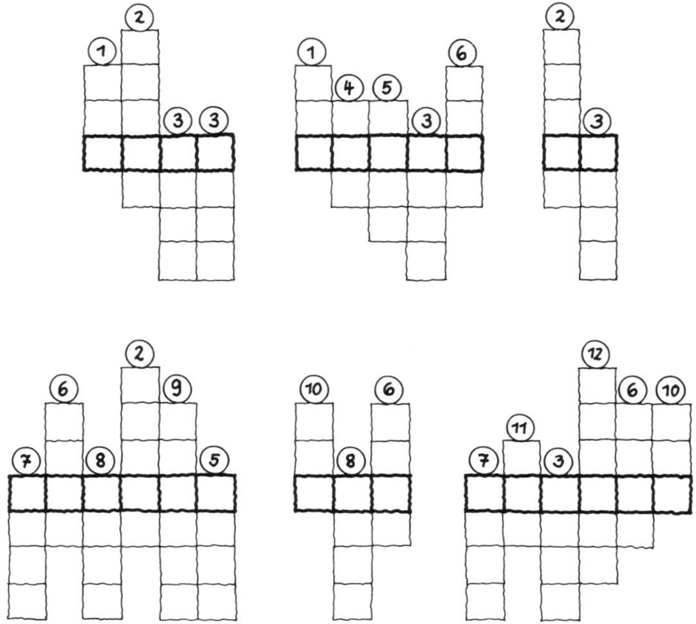

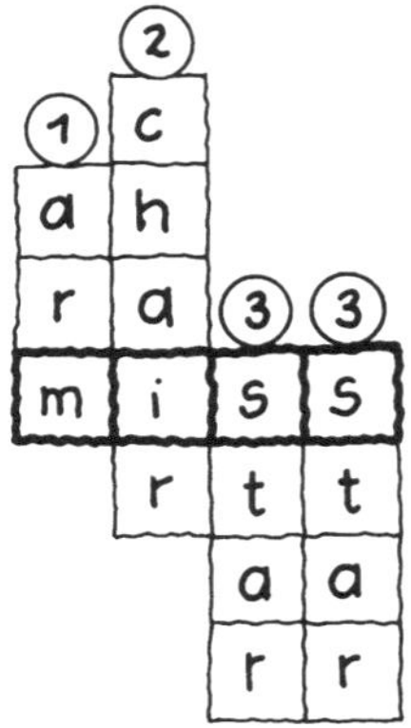
1 arm
2 chair
3 star
3 star
miss

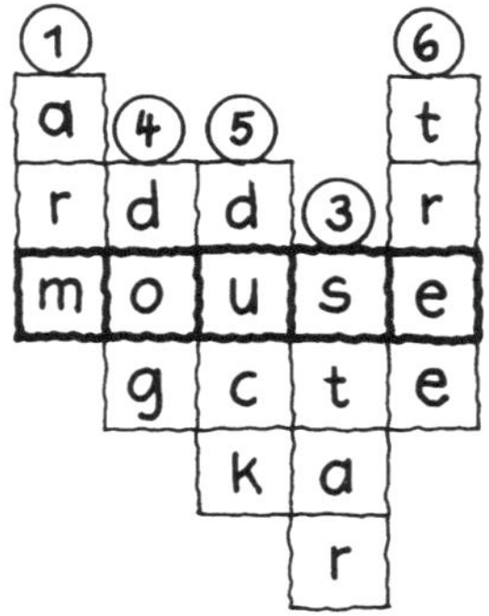
1 arm
4 dog
5 duck
3 star
6 tree
mouse

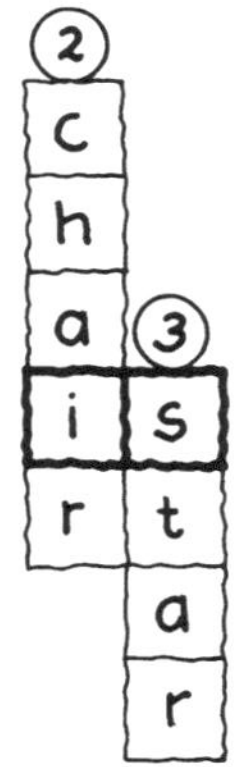
2 chair
3 star
is

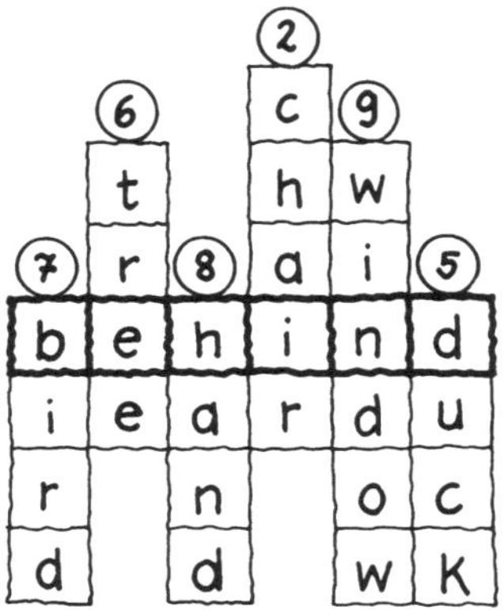
7 bird
6 tree
8 hand
2 chair
9 window
5 duck
behind

10 cat
8 hand
6 tree
the

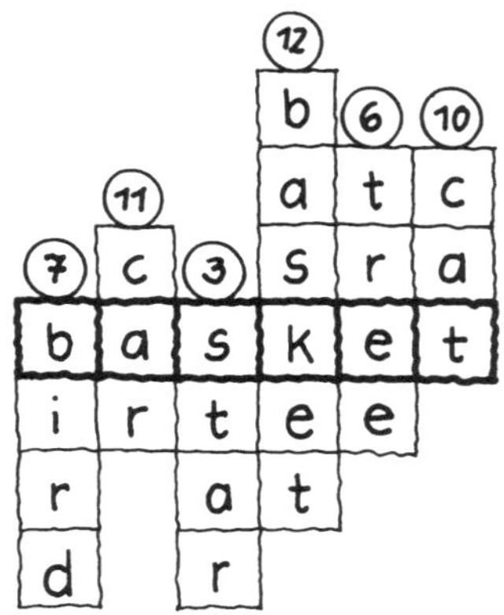
7 bird
11 car
3 star
12 basket
6 tree
10 cat
basket

Rhyming pictures

Von 3 Bildern reimt sich jeweils eins nicht. Streiche es durch!

banana (box – fox)
candle (boot – foot)
apple (bee – tree)
cake (moon – spoon)
bucket (boat – coat)
bicycle (star – car)
knife (hat – cat)
telephone (pen – hen)
ruler (cake – lake)

house (frog – dog)
book (shirt – skirt)
cow (map – cap)
pencil (house – mouse)
car (clock – sock)
bed (sun – gun)
football (key – ski)
flower (eight – plate)
hand (rose – nose)

At school

Dieses Rätsel hat 2 Teile. „Übersetze“ zuerst die Zahlen in Buchstaben und schreibe sie darunter, z. B.:

9	5	2	6	4	11
c	a	r	p	e	t

Verbinde dann jedes Wort mit dem passenden Bild!

2	3	8	8	4	2

6	4	7	9	12	1

2	3	1	4	2

9	13	5	12	2

6	3	6	12	1

10	5	11	9	13	4	1

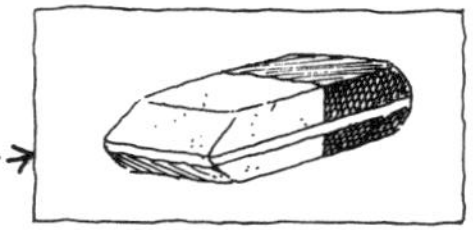
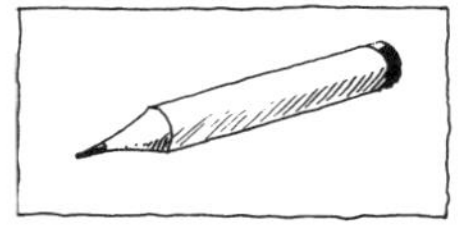

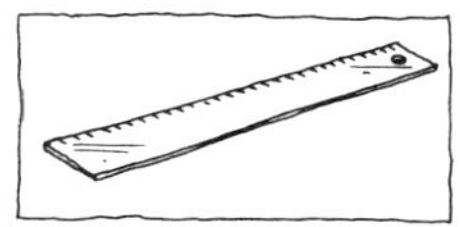

rubber
pencil
ruler
chair
pupil
satchel

Jobs

Schreibe den jeweiligen Beruf unter das passende Bild! Die Silben im Kasten helfen dir dabei.

far-	nur-	ba-	but-	post-	-mer
pi-	tea-	cap-	-lot	-cher	
-man	-se	-ker	-cher	-tain	

dentist

dentist
farmer
butcher

pilot
teacher
postman
nurse
baker
captain

A lot to see in our town

Lies die Wörter auf der rechten Seite und male diejenigen Felder mit Rotstift aus, in denen ein Begriff steht, den du im Bild sehen kannst.

flag	ball	star	table	man
sun	girl	zebra	tree	egg
lemon	frog	boy	moon	cup
knife	house	flower	car	spoon
woman	basket	ship	banana	street

Die ausgemalten Bilder ergeben zusammen einen Buchstaben. Welchen? Kreise ihn ein!

A X Z H S

Im Bild:

flag
man
girl
tree
boy
house
car
woman
street

Lösung: x

New words

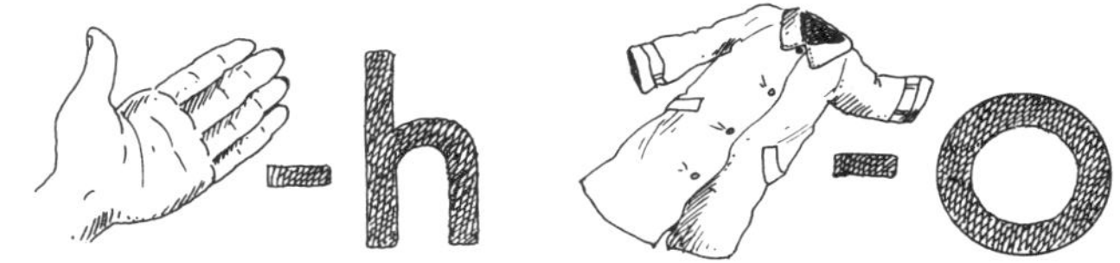

For example: hand - h = and

Numbers

Trage die ausgeschriebenen Zahlen in das Rätselgitter ein!

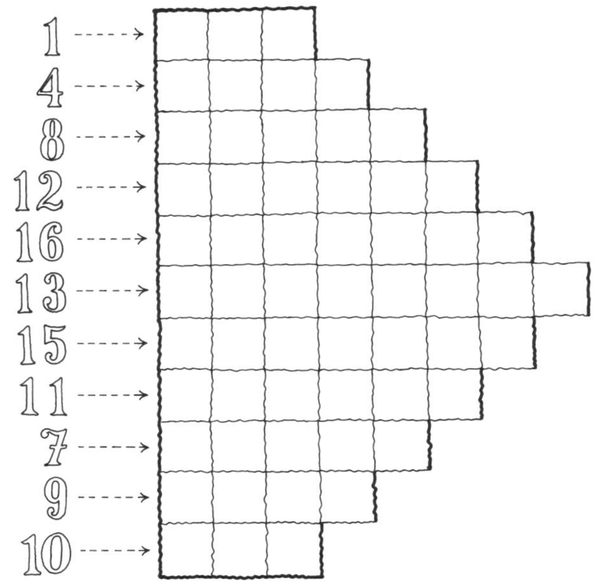

coat	–	o	=	cat
feather	–	e	=	father
brush	–	r	=	bush
frog	–	r	=	fog
ball	–	b	=	all
pear	–	p	=	ear
snail	–	s	=	nail

one
four
eight
twelve
sixteen
thirteen
fifteen
eleven
seven
nine
ten

If you add all the numbers,
you get 106.

Pictures and sentences

Schreibe in das Kästchen hinter jedem Satz den Erkennungsbuchstaben des dazugehörigen Bildes!

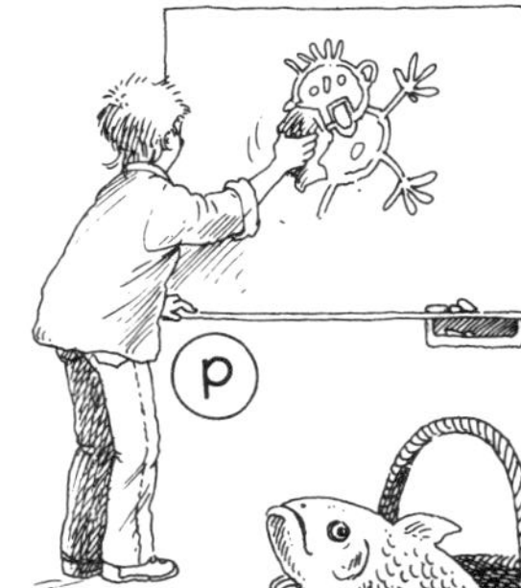

The cat is on the chair.

Mrs. Brown is reading the newspaper.

Tom is cleaning the board.

The fish is in the basket.

The mouse is riding a bike.

The monkey is eating a banana.

Chris is reading a book.

Lucy goes shopping.

The children are laughing.

Bob is drawing a fish.

The cat is on the chair.	S
Mrs. Brown is reading the newspaper.	U
Tom is cleaning the board.	P
The fish is in the basket.	E
The mouse is riding a bike.	R

The monkey is eating a banana.	G
Chris is reading a book.	R
Lucy goes shopping.	E
The children are laughing.	A
Bob is drawing a fish.	T

Picture crossword

Trage den Namen jedes abgebildeten Gegenstands in das Kreuzworträtsel ein!

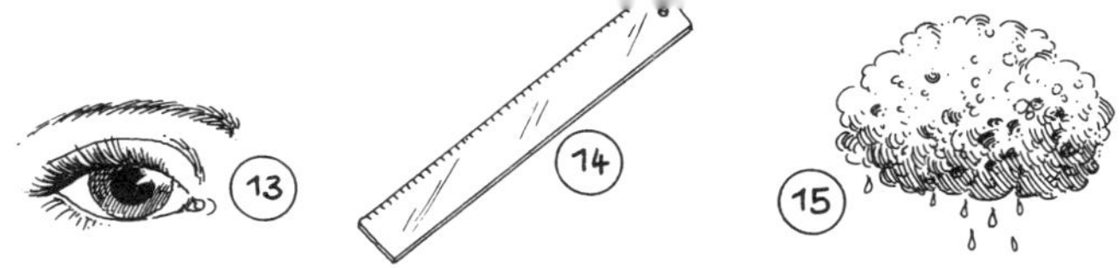

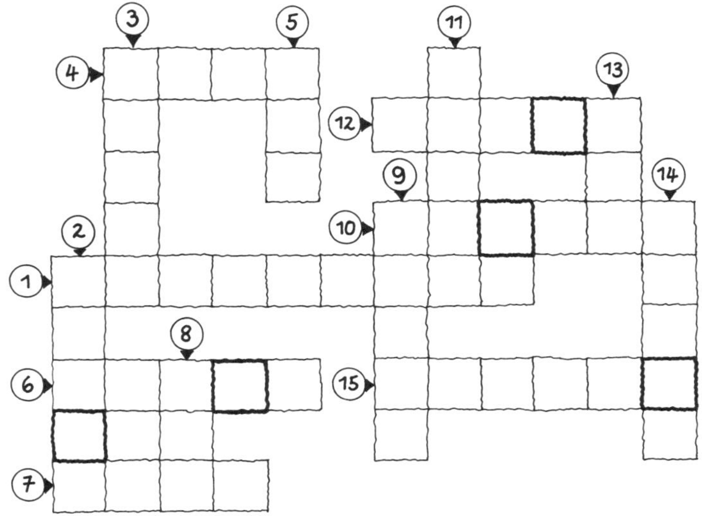

Wenn du die dick umrandeten Buchstaben hier einträgst, erhältst du das Lösungsmotto. Aufgepasst: Die richtige Reihenfolge der Buchstaben musst du noch finden!

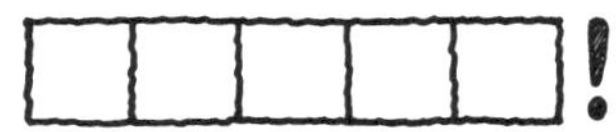

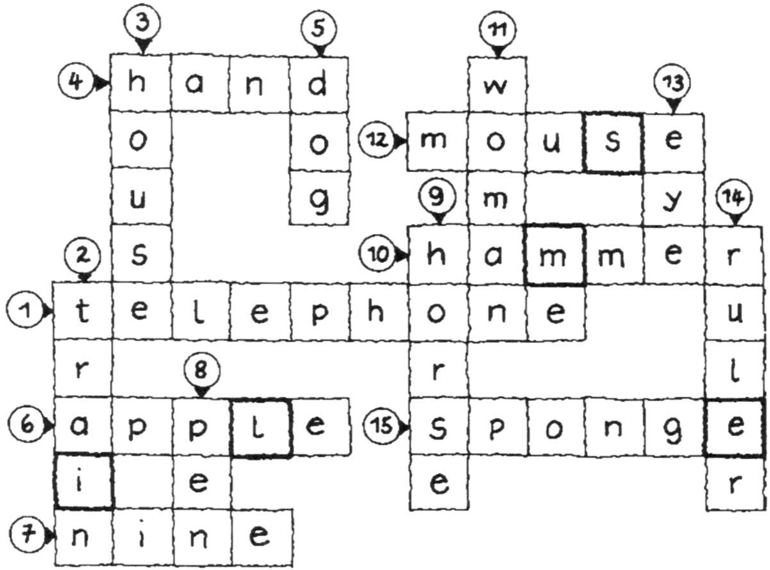

Lösung: smile!

Colours

Welche Farben haben die abgebildeten Dinge in Wirklichkeit? Trage die Farben ins Rätselgitter ein!

Male die Felder in den angegebenen Farben aus! Drehe das Bild um, wenn du fertig bist!

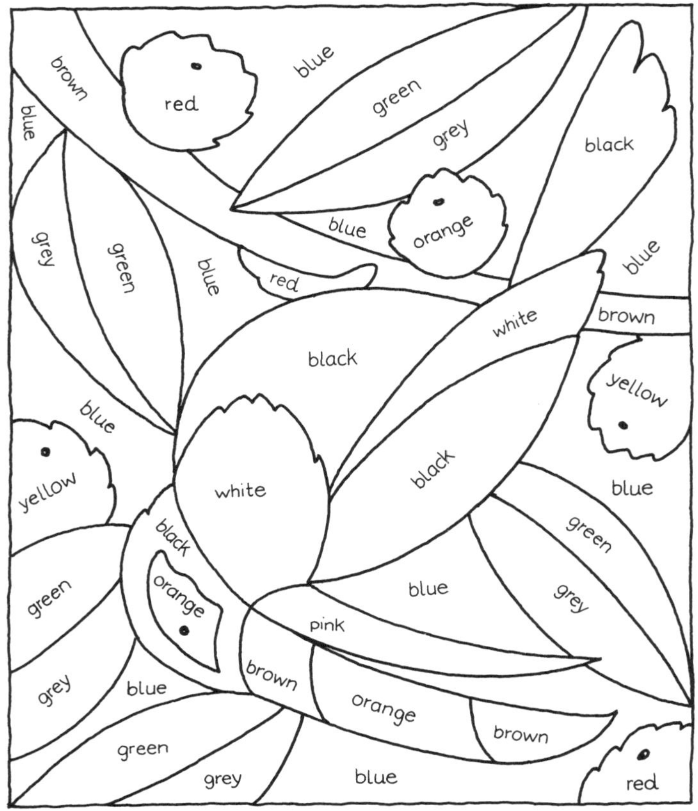

				r	e	d		
		o	r	a	n	g	e	
		w	h	i	t	e		
		p	i	n	k			
				b	l	a	c	k
y	e	l	l	o	w			
	b	r	o	w	n			

Lösung: rainbow

This bird is a toucan.

Complete the sentences!

Finde für jeden Satz die fehlende Präposition!

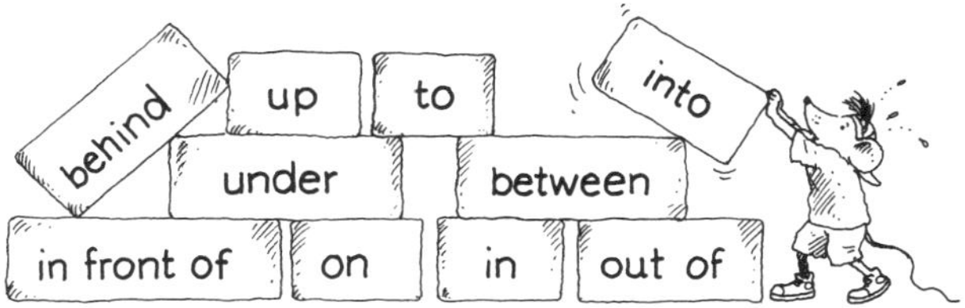

Miss Mouse is going ___________ school.

Miss Mouse is sitting ___________ a chair.

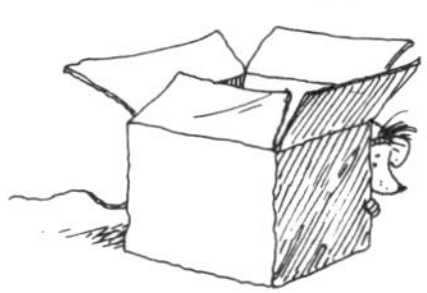

Miss Mouse is ___________ a box.

Miss Mouse is playing ___________ the garden.

Miss Mouse is climbing ___________ a ladder.

Miss Mouse is going ___________ the house.

Miss Mouse is standing ___________ two cats.

Miss Mouse is reading ___________ the table.

Miss Mouse is looking ___________ the tent.

Miss Mouse is ___________ the shop.

Miss Mouse is going to school.
Miss Mouse is sitting on a chair.
Miss Mouse is behind a box.
Miss Mouse is playing in the garden.

Miss Mouse is climbing up a ladder.
Miss Mouse is going into the house.
Miss Mouse is standing between two cats.
Miss Mouse is reading under the table.
Miss Mouse is looking out of the tent.
Miss Mouse is in front of the shop.